MY FINGERS
ARE FOR TOUCHING

Library of Congress Cataloging-in-Publication Data
Moncure, Jane Belk.
My fingers are for touching / Jane Belk-Moncure;
illustrated by Viki Woodworth.
p. cm.
Summary: Illustrates the many different kinds of textures which fingers can touch and feel as well as some of the other things they can do.
ISBN 1-56766-284-6

1. Touch — Juvenile literature. 2. Fingers — Juvenile literature. [1. Touch. 2. Fingers. 3. Senses and sensations.] I. Woodworth, Viki, ill. II. Title.
QP451.M69 1997   97-815
612.88 — dc21   CIP
                                                  AC

MY FINGERS ARE FOR TOUCHING

BY JANE BELK-MONCURE / ILLUSTRATED BY VIKI WOODWORTH

My fingers are for
touching furry things
like bunnies

that wiggle their noses,

4

and fluffy
kittens soft and warm.

My fingers are for
touching

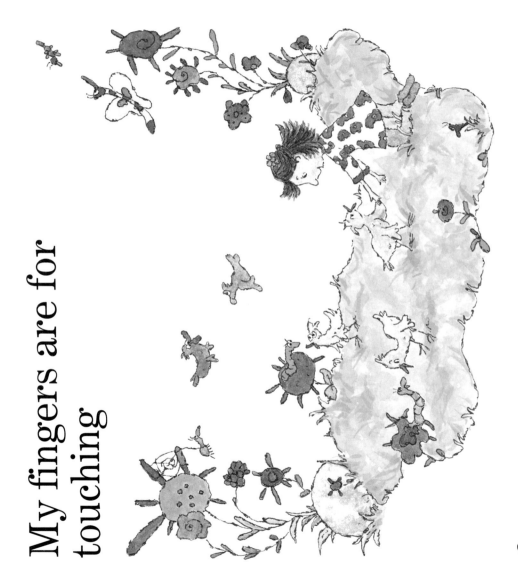

fuzzy
baby chicks

6

and a sleepy puppy that
curls up in my arms.

Sometimes I touch
lumpy things

like clay that I squeeze into
a crocodile, or a hill of sand
that turns into a castle.

My fingers touch rough tough things like a tree when I climb it or a big rock when I try to pick it up.

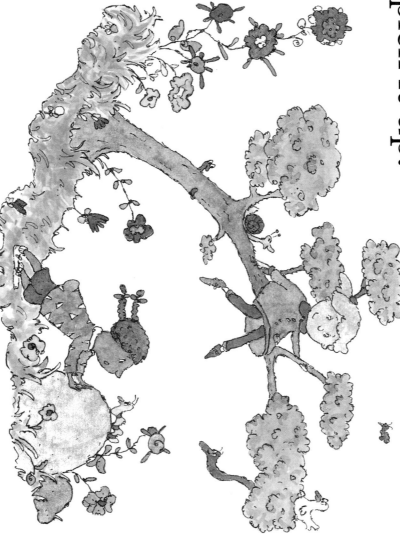

Sometimes I touch
smooth things

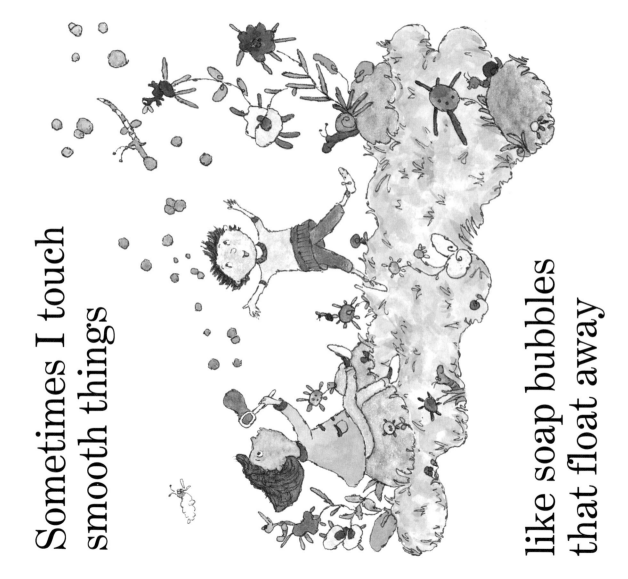

like soap bubbles
that float away

or a little green frog
that slips through
my fingers.

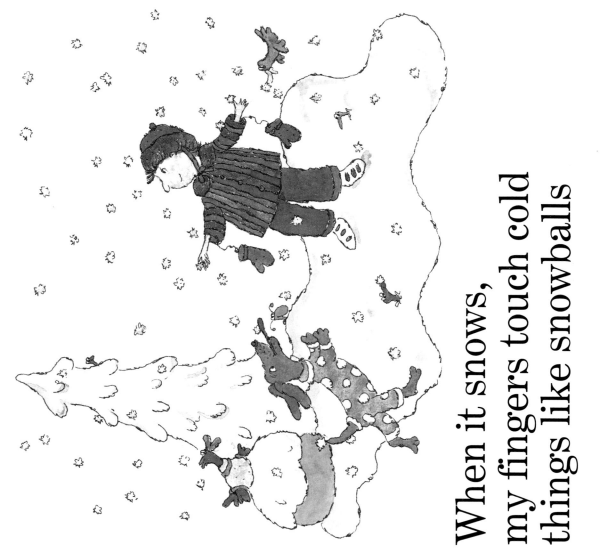

When it snows,
my fingers touch cold
things like snowballs

and warm things like
a cup of cocoa with a
marshmallow on top.

When I walk into the woods I
touch prickly pine cones

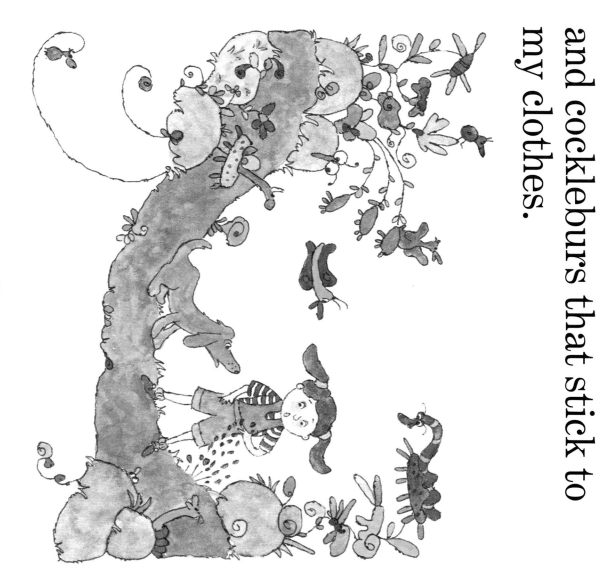

and cockleburs that stick to
my clothes.

15

My fingers are
for helping too.

They help me build a
boat and sail it far away.

My fingers help me
make music.

They help me make a kite
and fly it in the sky.

My fingers help me catch a
ball and throw it to a friend.

They help me cut and
sew and tie a bow.

19

My fingers help me push my
sister in the swing.

They help me hold her up so she can see the big parade.

Sometimes I touch
with one finger.
I tickle with
both my hands.

Sometimes I use both arms
to stretch way out and give
a hug.